Exploring Latino Cultures Through Crafts

Mia Farrell

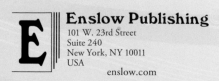

Enslow Publishing
101 W. 23rd Street
Suite 240
New York, NY 10011
USA

enslow.com

Published in 2016 by Enslow Publishing, LLC.
101 W. 23rd Street, Suite 240, New York, NY 10011

Cataloging-in-Publication Data
Farrell, Mia.
Exploring Latino cultures through crafts / by Mia Farrell.
p. cm. —(Multicultural crafts)
Includes bibliographical references and index.
ISBN 978-0-7660-6779-0 (library binding)
ISBN 978-0-7660-6777-6 (pbk.)
ISBN 98-0-7660-6778-3 (6-pack)
1. Handicraft — Latin America — Juvenile literature. 2. Handicraft — Juvenile literature. I. Title.
TT27.5 F377 2016
745.5089'68073—d23

Printed in the United States of America

To Our Readers: We have done our best to make sure all Web site addresses in this book were active and appropriate when we went to press. However, the author and the publisher have no control over and assume no liability for the material available on those Web sites or on any Web sites they may link to. Any comments or suggestions can be sent by e-mail to customerservice@enslow.com.

Portions of this book originally appeared in the book *Hispanic-American Crafts Kids Can Do!* by Fay Robinson .

Photo Credits: Crafts prepared by June Ponte; craft photography by Lindsay Pries. Andra Simionescu/Digital Vision Vectors/Getty Images (background thoughout book); De Agostini Picture Library/Getty Images, p. 24; Dioscoro Teofilo de la Puebla Tolin/Getty Images, p. 4; Fotosearch/Getty Images, p. 6; Gabrielle & Michel Therin-Weise/Robert Harding World Imagery/Getty Images, p. 10; Glow Images/Getty Images, p. 16; Gold Stock Images/Shutterstock.com, p. 14; Image Source/Getty Images, p. 22; Jennifer Broadus/Photolibrary/Getty Images, p. 18; John & Lisa Merrill/Photodisc/Getty Images, p. 5; Kevin Schafer/The Image Bank/Getty Images, p. 12; mileswork/Shutterstock.com, p. 1 (Earth icon);Robert Alexander/Archive Photos/Getty Images, p. 20; Wolfgang Kaehler/LightRocket via Getty Images, p. 8.

Cover Credits: Crafts prepared by June Ponte; craft photography by Lindsay Pries. Andra Simionescu/Digital Vision Vectors/Getty Images (background); mileswork/Shutterstock.com (Earth icon).

CONTENTS

Latino Cultures and Crafts 4

Ojo de Dios (God's Eye) 6

Mayan Woven Bookmark 8

Migajón Figurines 10

Mola From the Kuna 12

Headdress for Carnival 14

Mexican Talavera Pottery 16

Colorful Maracas 18

Huichol Yarn Art 20

Parrot Piñata 22

Mesoamerican Codex 24

Patterns 26

Learn More 30

Web Sites 31

Index 32

Safety Note: *Be sure to ask for help from an adult, if needed, to complete these crafts!*

Latino Cultures and Crafts

Christopher Columbus set sail across the Atlantic in 1492 in search of a passage from Europe to Asia. Instead, he discovered a new world. In this rugged land, Indian groups had thrived for thousands of years. Aztec, Maya, and Inca people had rich cultures. They developed dazzling architecture, massive stone sculptures, beautiful pottery, and colorful weavings. Many of their crafts were useful. Some served religious purposes.

Soldiers from Spain, called conquistadores, were sent to what is now Mexico and Peru to explore the New World. These soldiers conquered the native peoples in the name of their king, in search of gold.

The Spanish and the Portuguese settled the lands

Chistopher Columbus

4

Peru was once home to the Inca people who made colorful weavings from soft llama hair.

south of what is now the United States, an area called Latin America. Some people that live in these lands call themselves Hispanic, meaning "of or from Spain or Portugal." Others prefer to describe themselves as Latino or Latina.

During the rule of the Spanish and Portuguese, traditional arts and crafts were restricted. But after many revolutions for independence from European rule, traditional customs and crafts became more commonplace. Many craftsmen combined European and Native styles, creating a new form of craftsmanship that is unique to that part of the world.

Ojo de Dios (God's Eye)

This decoration is a tradition among the Pueblo peoples of northern Mexico. It is a symbol of seeing and understanding, and is often thought to be good luck.

The Pueblo tribes created apartment-like complexes made from adobe mud and stone.

What You Will Need

- glue
- 2 craft sticks
- yarn in 2 or 3 different colors
- scissors
- feathers (optional)
- beads (optional)

1. Glue two craft sticks together to make an X and let dry.

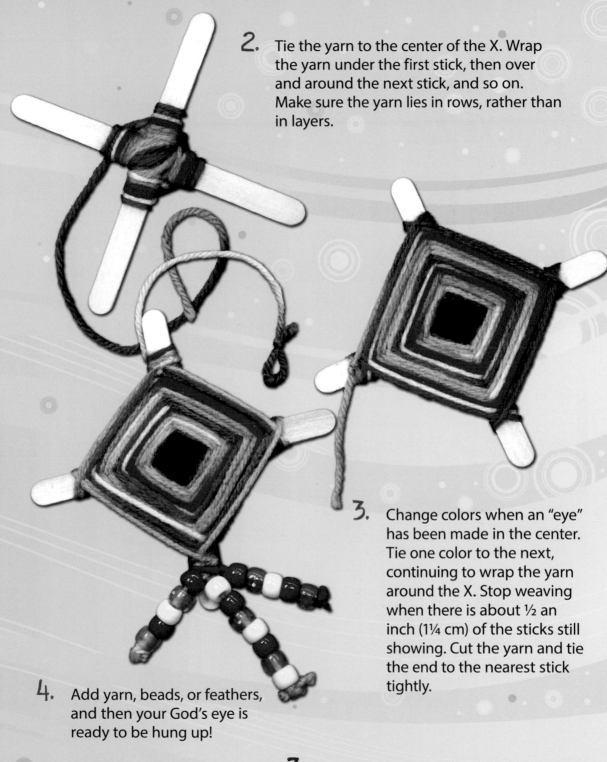

2. Tie the yarn to the center of the X. Wrap the yarn under the first stick, then over and around the next stick, and so on. Make sure the yarn lies in rows, rather than in layers.

3. Change colors when an "eye" has been made in the center. Tie one color to the next, continuing to wrap the yarn around the X. Stop weaving when there is about ½ an inch (1¼ cm) of the sticks still showing. Cut the yarn and tie the end to the nearest stick tightly.

4. Add yarn, beads, or feathers, and then your God's eye is ready to be hung up!

7

Mayan Woven Bookmark

Mythology states that the goddess Ixchel taught the first woman to weave at the beginning of time. Since then, the Maya people of Guatemala have become known for their brightly-colored tapestries. They are made into clothing, bags, tablecloths and wall hangings. Make your own colorful woven bookmark.

Each village has a distinct pattern for their weaving.

What You Will Need

- ⊚ **colorful yarn**
- ⊚ **5 drinking straws**
- ⊚ **scissors**

1. To make a loom, thread a piece of yarn through each straw, leaving 2 to 3 inches (5 to 8 cm) sticking out of each end. Line up the straws and tie the yarn together.

2. Cut another piece of yarn 1 to 2 feet (about $1/3$ to $2/3$ meters) long. Tie one end to a straw.

3. Weave the yarn over and under each straw until you get to the other side of the loom. Then weave the yarn the other way. Continue weaving until you have about an inch ($2\frac{1}{2}$ cm) of yarn left.

4. Tie another 1-to-2-foot-long ($1/3$ to $2/3$ m) piece of yarn of a different color to the end of the last piece. Continue weaving.

5. When you have reached the end of the straws, tie off the yarn around the end of the straw.

6. Untie the knot of yarn and carefully remove the straws. Tie the knot again, and your weaving is done!

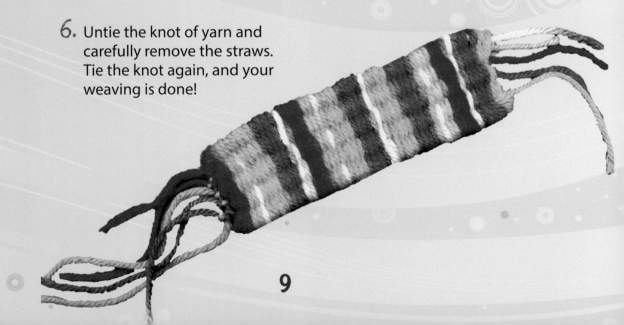

Migajón Figurines

Migajón is a type of dough used to make toys and figurines throughout Central and South America. Make your own version of this clay by using white bread and glue.

Dough figurines are commonly sold as decorations.

What You Will Need

- 🌀 1 slice of white bread for each figurine
- 🌀 small bowl
- 🌀 white glue
- 🌀 tablespoon
- 🌀 paintbrush
- 🌀 poster paints

1. After removing the crust, tear a piece of soft white bread into pieces and place them in a bowl.

2. Pour one tablespoon (15 ml) of white glue over the breadcrumbs.

3. Use your fingers to mix the glue and the bread. As the glue mixes in, tear the bread into smaller and smaller pieces, continuing to mix. After a few minutes, the mixture will feel like wet clay.

4. Use the clay to form small animals or toys. Let the figures dry completely, which may take a day or two.

5. Paint the figures with bright colors.

MOLA FROM THE KUNA

Molas are panels of colorful fabric created by the women of the Kuna Indians in Panama. In fact, the word mola means "blouse" in the native Kuna tongue. Shapes are cut through layers of different colored cloth. These make beautiful decorations. You can create a mola effect with paper or felt.

A mola's quality is determined by the number of layers and the fineness of the stitching.

WHAT YOU WILL NEED

- pencil or pen
- 3 brightly colored pieces of construction paper or felt
- scissors
- glue

1. Draw the outline of a simple design on a dark piece of paper or felt. (See page 28 for a bird pattern.) Carefully cut out the design from the center out, leaving the paper or felt in one piece.

2. Place a second, different colored piece of paper or felt under the first. Draw the details of the design on the second piece, and then cut those out.

3. Layer the first piece of paper or felt over the second piece and glue them together. Then, layer these on top of another piece or paper or felt of a different color. Line up the edges and glue in place.

HEADDRESS FOR CARNIVAL

Every February, the country of Brazil throws a huge party called Carnival. Carnival was originally a festival marking the beginning of Lent, when people would have to keep from dancing and singing. Now it is a time to celebrate life and the coming of spring. In Brazil blocos, or parades, take up entire streets with people wearing bright costumes and dancing to loud music.

The headdresses worn for Carnival are big and colorful.

WHAT YOU WILL NEED

- pencil
- poster board
- scissors
- stapler or tape
- glue
- markers
- glitter
- sequins
- craft feathers
- ribbon

1. Fold a large piece of paper in half. The fold should line up with the wider part of the pattern. Using the template on page 27, trace the headdress onto paper, then onto poster board. Cut it out.

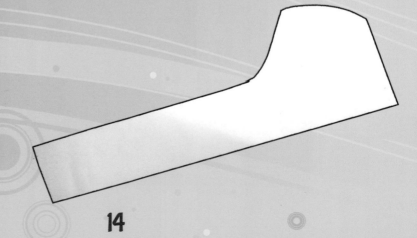

2. Have someone help you hold it around your head, overlapping the ends as needed to make it fit. Take it off while holding the ends together, and staple or tape them together.

3. Use glitter, sequins, ribbons, feathers, dried flowers or leaves, and markers to decorate your headdress.

MEXICAN TALAVERA POTTERY

Created by hand in Puebla, Mexico, talavera pottery is made from terra cotta, a rust-colored clay which is sculpted, heated, and then painted with bright colors. The plates, bowls, vases, and pitchers are beautiful and can be used every day. Brighten up your home with talavera pottery!

The process used to make talavera pottery has been the same for hundreds of years.

WHAT YOU WILL NEED

- ☺ terra cotta clay or air-drying modeling clay
- ☺ water
- ☺ paintbrush
- ☺ poster paint

1. Make a ball of clay by rolling it in your palms. Stick your thumbs into the center of the ball. With your fingers, press the sides up, trying to keep the pot's walls the same thickness all the way up and around. To keep the clay from cracking, use water.

2. Gently press and pull on the walls of the pot until you get the shape you want. You could add a handle, a spout, or even a lid. Let the clay pot dry.

3. Decorate with brightly colored poster paint.

17

Colorful Maracas

Maracas are common percussion instruments in Latin American bands. They give off a distinct rhythmic sound. They were originally made from dried gourds with seeds inside to make a rattling sound. Here's a way to make maracas without waiting for gourds to dry.

Maracas are used in salsa music.

What You Will Need

- uncooked rice, pasta, or dried peas
- a clean, empty plastic salad dressing bottle
- paintbrush
- poster paint
- colorful tissue paper
- white glue

1. Put some uncooked rice, pasta, or dried peas into a clean, dry salad dressing bottle. Twist the cap on tightly.

2. Paint a thin layer of glue over the bottle and apply scraps of tissue paper. Cover the whole bottle. Paint glue over the paper and allow it to dry.

3. To seal the cap on the bottle, cover the gap with tissue paper and glue. Let dry.

4. You can paint flowers, birds, or other designs onto the maraca. See the pattern on page 29 for inspiration.

HUICHOL YARN ART

The Huichol Indians of Mexico are known for their nieli'ka, or yarn art. These creations are made by pressing yarn into beeswax. They are used to tell stories about their history, traditions, and beliefs. Tell your own story with yarn.

Some of the yarn art patterns have been used for centuries.

WHAT YOU WILL NEED

- a 5-inch x 5-inch (13-cm x 13-cm) piece cardboard
- pencil
- white glue
- scissors
- yarn, many colors

1. Draw a design or picture on a piece of cardboard (or follow the pattern on page 26).

2. Squeeze a line of glue over the lines of your drawing on the cardboard. Then, place a piece of yarn over the glue, holding it in place with the pencil. For curved lines, you may find it helpful to hold the yarn in place for a couple of minutes until the glue dries a little before continuing.

3. Fill in the shape with different colors of yarn until the cardboard is filled. You could also have simple line designs in the remaining space.

Parrot Piñata

Piñatas are a fun Latin American tradition. They are often shaped like animals and made of colorfully painted papier maché. Children take turns hitting the piñata. When it breaks open, candy or small toys rain on party guests. Make a piñata for your next party!

Piñatas are a great party activity!

What You Will Need

- a balloon
- 1 cup (225 g) flour
- 2 cups (473 ml) water
- newspaper, cut into 1-inch (2½ cm) strips
- a mixing bowl
- poster paints
- scissors
- masking tape
- yarn or twine
- candy or small toys
- craft feathers
- craft foam

1. Blow up the balloon and tie it closed.

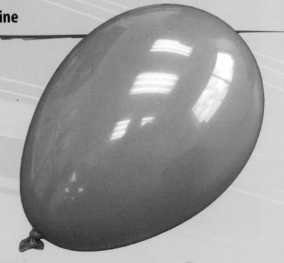

2. Mix flour and water together in a bowl. Dip strips of newspaper into the mixture and carefully cover the balloon with the wet newspaper strips. Leave an area of about 1 inch (2½ cm).

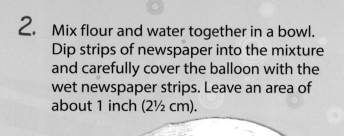

3. Tie a piece of yarn about 8 feet (2½ m) long around the middle of the balloon. This will be used to hang up the finished piñata. Cover the balloon and string with three to four more layers of newspaper dipped in the flour mixture. Let the piñata dry. This may take a day or two.

4. Pop the balloon. Put candy or small toys in the opening, then tape it closed.

5. Paint the whole piñata with bright colors. Add colored foam to make a beak for the bird. You can also add feathers to make wings. Let dry.

PATTERNS

The percentages included on the patterns tell you how much to enlarge or shrink the image using a copier. Most copiers and printers have an adjustable size/percentage feature to change the size of an image when you print it. After you print the pattern to its correct size, cut it out. Trace it onto the material listed in the craft.

Yarn Art

At 100%

Carnival Headdress

Enlarge by 165%

Molas

Enlarge by 115%

Flower Pattern for
Maracas

At 100%

Learn More

Carlson, Lori Marie. *Cool Salsa: Bilingual Poems on Growing Up Latino in the United States.* New York: Square Fish Publishing, 2013.

Maloy, Jackie. *The Ancient Maya.* Chicago: Children's Press, 2010.

Palmer, Bill. *Latino Folklore and Culture.* Broomall, Penn.: Mason Crest Publishing, 2013.

Petrillo, Valerie. *A Kid's Guide to Latino History: More than 50 Activities.* Chicago: Chicago Review Press, 2009.

WEB SITES

**scholastic.com/teachers/collection/
bring-hispanic-heritage-month-life-collection-resources**
Click through links to discover more about Hispanic heritage.

enchantedlearning.com/crafts/mexico/
Make Mexican crafts.

ducksters.com/history/maya/art.php
Learn about the different kinds of art created by the Maya.

INDEX

A
Asia, 4
Aztec Indians, 4, 24

B
balloons, 22–23
beads, 6–7
beeswax, 20
bookmark, 8–9
Brazil, 14
bread, 10–11

C
cardboard, 20–21
Carnival, 14, 27
clay, 10–11, 16
clear tape, 24
codex, 24
Columbus, Christopher, 4
conquistadores, 14
construction paper, 12
craft
    foam, 22
    sticks, 6

E
Europe, 4–5

F
fabric, 12
feathers, 6–7, 14–15, 22
felt, 12–13

G
glitter, 14–15
glue, 6, 10, 12–14, 18–21
glyphs, 24
gourds, 18
Guatemala, 8

H
headdress, 14–15, 27
Hispanic, 5
Huichol Indians, 20

I
Incan Indians, 4
index cards, 24
Ixchel, 8

K
Kuna Indians, 12

M
maracas, 18–19, 29
markers, 14–15, 24–25
masking tape, 22
Mayan Indians, 4, 8
Mexico, 4–6, 16, 20, 24
migajón, 10
mola, 12, 28

P
Panama, 12
parades, 14
patterns, 26–29

pencil, 12, 14, 20–21, 24
Peru, 5
piñata, 22–23
Portugal, 5
poster
    board, 14
    paint, 10, 16–18, 22
pottery, 4, 16

R
ribbon, 14–15

S
scissors, 6, 8, 12, 14, 20, 22
sequins, 14–15
Spain, 4–5
straws, 8–9

T
terra cotta, 16
tissue paper, 18–19

Y
yarn, 6–7, 8–9, 20–22